Knitted Deer Slippers

by

Janis Frank

I've always wanted to design a pair of slippers that had a bit more character and substance—something that not only looks good but fits snugly and keeps you cozy. The deer motif on top of the foot gives these slippers a rustic charm, while the substantial cuff provides extra warmth and a secure fit. These slippers are great for knitters who are comfortable with basic stitches and ready to dive into something a bit more intricate.

This pattern is packed with various cable stitches, so you'll get plenty of practice with your cable needle. The cables vary—sometimes you'll be knitting the stitches on the cable needle, sometimes purling, and the number of stitches will also change. To keep things simple, I explain how to work each cable stitch as you go along, so you won't need to constantly check the *Abbreviations* section.

This isn't a beginner pattern, but if you're familiar with the basics of knitting and feel comfortable using a cable needle, you'll be able to handle this. I've included lots of helpful photos to guide you through the deer motif, so you'll have plenty of visual aids as you knit.

Table of Contents

Things You Need

1 ball of worsted weight yarn (average 260 yard, 5 oz or 141 gram ball will be more than enough)

2 sets of size 4 mm (US size 6) single point knitting needles.

Stitch holder

Cable Needle

Tapestry needle to sew in ends. You can also use this handy video tutorial to show you how to work in the ends while knitting these slippers.

Gauge

With size 4 mm (US size 6) needles or *whatever size you need* to obtain the correct number of stitches and rows. Be sure to check your gauge otherwise the sizing won't be correct.

In *garter stitch*

2" = 9 sts

2" = 18 rows

Sizes (are written as such)

Women's 6-7 (**8-9,** 10-11, **12-13**)

Men's 5-6 (**7-8,** 9-10, **11-12**)

Toe Flap

Cast on 14 sts

✋**Row 1**: P across

Row 2: K across ✋

Repeat from ✋ to ✋ 2 (**3**, 4, **5**) times *more* for a total of 6 (**8**, 10, **12**) rows

Next Row: P6 K2 P6

Next Row: K5 Pick up the next st with the cable needle. Pull the st FORWARD, P the next st. P the st on the cable needle. Pick up the next st with the cable needle. Pull the st BACK, P the next st. P the st on the cable needle. K5

✪**Next Row**: P5 K4 P5

Next Row: K5 P4 K5 ✪ Repeat from ✪ to ✪ one more time

Next Row: P4 Pick up the next st with the cable needle. Pull the st BACK, K the next st. K the st on the cable needle. K2 Pick up the next st with the cable needle. Pull the st FORWARD, K the next st. K the st on the cable needle. P4

Next Row: K4 P6 K4

Next Row: P4 K6 P4

Next Row: K4 P6 K4

Next Row: P3 Pick up the next st with the cable needle. Pull the st BACK, K the next 2 sts. K the st on the cable needle. K2 Pick up the next 2 sts with the cable needle. Pull the st FORWARD, K the next st. K the 2 sts on the cable needle. P3

Next Row: K3 P8 K3

Next Row: P3 K2 P1 K1 PM1 K1 P1 K2 P3 (15 sts)

Next Row: K3 P2 K1 P1 K1 M1 P1 K1 P2 K3 (16 sts)

Next Row: P3 K2tog (When making this stitch, pick up a stitch as if to knit. Twist the stitch and place it back on your non-working needle. Knit the 2 stitches together from right to left.) P1 K1 P2 K1 P1 K2tog (as you normally would left to right) P3 (14 sts)

Scan this QR code for help with
the first K2tog in this row

Next Row: K5 P1 K2 P1 K5

Next Row: P4 Pick up the next st with the cable needle. Pull the st BACK, K1 in the st BELOW (see photos). P1 the st on the cable needle. K1 P2 **_K1_** P1 K1 in the 2nd st BELOW (knit this st in the knit st you made before the P1 as shown in the photos). P4 (16 sts)

Knit in the stitch below

Pull up a loop knit-wise like this.

After purling the st from the cable needle,
knit the next st on your non-working needle

The other antler.
You already knitted the st so it needs to be
2 sts down as shown. This is the st that is
bold and italicized in the pattern.

Pick up this st with the non-working needle.

Branch of second antler complete.

Next Row: K4 P1 K1 P1 K2 P1 K1 P1 K4

Next Row: P3 Pick up the next st with the cable needle. Pull the st BACK, K the next st. P the st on the cable needle. P1 K1 P2 K1 P1 Pick up the next st with the cable needle. Pull the st FORWARD, P the next st. K the st on the cable needle. P3

Next Row: K3 P1 K2 P1 K2 P1 K2 P1 K3

Next Row: P2 Pick up the next st with the cable needle. Pull the st BACK, K the next st. P the st on the cable needle. P8 Pick up the next st with the cable needle. Pull the st FORWARD, P the next st. K the st on the cable needle. P2

Next Row: K2 P1 K10 P1 K2

♦**Next Row**: P across

Next Row: K16 ♦ Repeat from ♦ to ♦ 1 (**2**, 3, **4**) times *more*. If you want a different colour for the cuff, break yarn when the last row is completed.

Making the Cuff

Next Row:(with the optional cuff colour) K16. Cast on an additional 11 (**12**, 13, **14**). You now have 27 (**28**, 29, **30**) sts on your needle.

Next Row: K27 (**28**, 29, **30**). Cast on an additional 11 (**12**, 13, **14**). You now have 38 (**40**, 42, **44**) sts on your needle.

Next Rows: K across for a total of 13 (**15**, 17, **19**) rows.

Next Row: With the WRONG side facing you, P across.

⌘ ☺ **Next Row**: With the RIGHT side facing you, (K1 P2) across. Maintain this pattern with any remaining sts at the end of the row.

Next Row: K across. ⌘ Repeat from ⌘ to ⌘ 6 (**7, 8, 9**) times *more*. For a total of 14 (**16**, 18, **20**) rows. Repeat the row marked with ☺ one more time.

Cast off *loosely* with the WRONG side facing you.

If you would like to change the colour around the toe and foot, change colour now.

Sides of Foot

This is where you're going to need the extra set of knitting needles. You'll be knitting back and forth in rows but the turn around the toe is too tight to use circular needles. For this, you'll put the 13 toe flap stitches on one of your extra needles. It's a little unconventional, but it works.

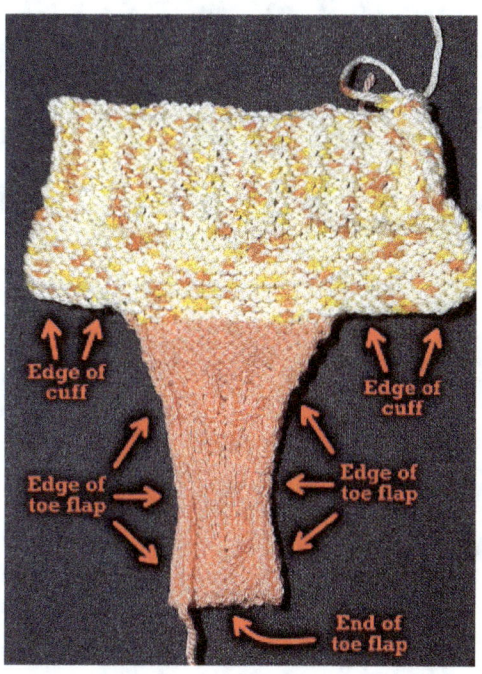

The sections of the slipper.

Next Row: With the *RIGHT* side facing, pick up 11 (**12,** 13, **14**) stitches evenly along the edge of the cuff and place onto one of your needles. Pick up 18 (**20,** 22, **24**) stitches evenly along the edge of the toe flap. (All of these stitches are on *ONE* needle. (29, **32,** 35, **38**) stitches on this needle)

With another needle, pick up 13 stitches evenly along the end of the toe flap.

With another needle, pick up 18 (**20,** 22, **24**) stitches evenly along the side of the toe flap. Pick up 11 (**12,** 13, **14**) stitches evenly along the edge of the cuff and place onto the next needle. (29, **32,** 35, **38**) stitches on this needle)

You should now have 3 needles holding stitches with all the points pointing as shown below when laid flat. You also have one spare needle to knit with. You are now going to knit in rows, back and forth with these three needles. Once you finish knitting all the stitches on one needle, move on to the next needle (the point of the needle is right there) until you complete the row.

I used a capped double pointed needle to work my 13 stitches
for the end of the toe. A regular needle also works.

Knit the next 8 (**10,** 10, **12**) rows

There are 4 (**5,** 5, **6**) ridges on the tip of the toe.

The following photo shows the 5 ridges for the women's size 8-9 or the men's 7-8.

These are the ridges picked up along the side.

Next Row: With **WRONG** side facing. Cast off all the stitches from the first needle *loosely*. You'll need to pass the last stitch from the first needle over the first stitch of the toe flap stitches (second needle).

Using the same needle that now has one stitch, knit the remaining 12 stitches of the toe flap. Cast off all the stitches from the third needle *loosely*. Break yarn.

Making the Sole

If you need more help than the photos provide, you can watch the how-to video by taking a pic of the QR code below or by using this link - https://bit.ly/knit-the-sole
Both the link and the QR code start the video in the correct section. No need to find the spot. I already have it cued up for you.

Next Row: With the **RIGHT** side facing, attach yarn and knit the first stitch of the cast off stitches by the toe flap (cast off stitch on the right by the point of the needle).

Pick up this stitch at the start of the row.

K2tog. Knit to the last 2 stitches K2tog. Pick up the cast off stitch by the point of your needle. (13 stitches).

Pick up this stitch at the end of the row.

Quick tip – wrap the yarn counterclockwise around your needle and turn it down to pull the yarn through the cast off stitch on the right. If you have a hard time doing this, you can also use a crochet hook to pull the loop through and place that loop on your working needle.

You now are working back and forth along the bottom of the foot picking up one cast off stitch on each side as you go.

Next Row: Knit across.

ʤ Next Row: Pick up the next stitch of the cast off stitches. K2tog. Knit to the last 2 stitches K2tog. Pick up the cast off stitch on the other side of the slipper by the point of your needle. (13 stitches).

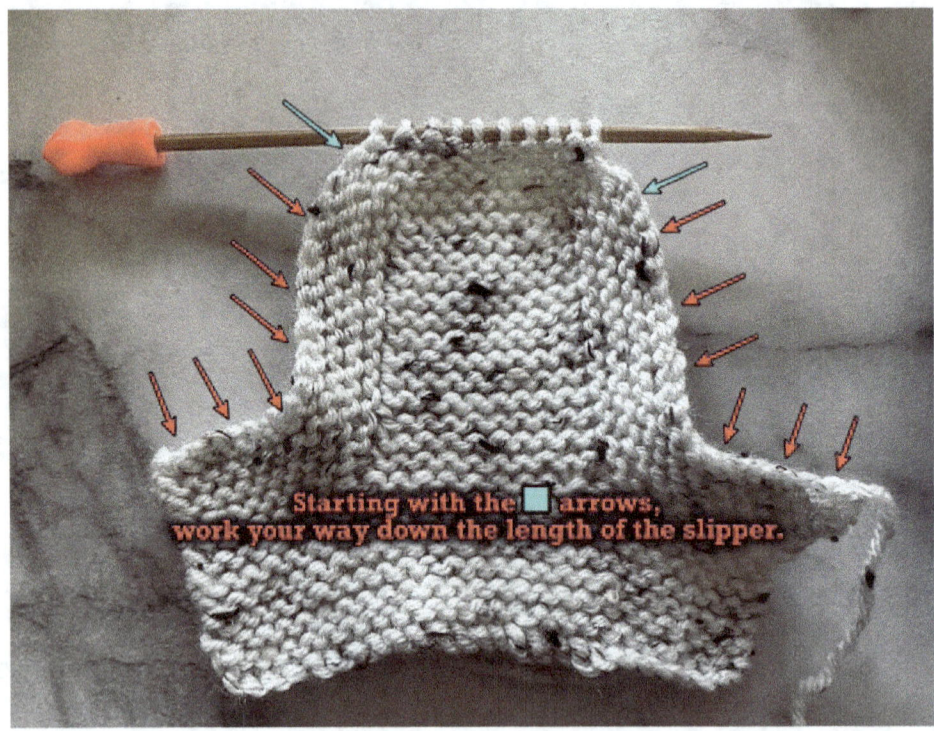

Next Row: Knit across **ʤ**

Repeat from **ʤ** to **ʤ** down the entire length of the foot. There are equal number of cast off stitches along each side. How many rows varies depending on the size of slipper you're making. Be sure to end with a completed knit across row.

Starting the sole. Right side.

Working your way down while making the sole. Wrong side.

Continuing to work down the length of the sole

Still further down the sole. Note how the cast off edges are being picked up as you go.
Keep working your way down the length of the sole until you've picked up all the cast off stitches.

Take a photo of this square for
FREE knitting pattens on my website!

Making the Heel

If you need more help than the photos provide, you can watch the how-to video by taking a pic of the QR code below or by using this link - https://bit.ly/knit-the-heel

Both the link and the QR code start the video in the correct section. No need to find the spot. I already have it cued up for you.

You're now going to make a small triangle to fit in the back of the heel. You're going to fill this space in the slipper.

◖ Next Row: With the **RIGHT** side facing, pick up a stitch in the row closest to the sole of the slipper. Count how many ridges it is for the size you are making. K2tog twice. Knit to the last 4 stitches. K2tog twice. Count down the same number of ridges on the other side and pick up a stitch in the space beneath it. (11 stitches).

The photo above shows 9 rows of ridges.
These are rows you knit to form the edges of the slipper.

Stitch picked up on the right edge in the 9th row shown above

After you K2tog at the end of the row, you'll pick up a stitch here.

Stitch picked up at the end of the row.

Next Row: Knit across.

Next Row: Count down one ridge less than the previous row and pick up a stitch in the space beneath it. K2tog. Knit until the last 2 stitches. K2tog. Count down the same number of ridges and pick up a stitch in the space beneath it on the other side.

Next Row: Knit across. ⓒ Repeat from ⓒ to ⓒ until 7 stitches remain. End with the K across row.

Next Row: Count down one ridge less than the previous row and pick up a stitch in the space beneath it. K2tog. K3tog. K2tog. Count down the same number of ridges and pick up a stitch in the space beneath it on the other side.

Next Row: Knit across.

Next Row: K2tog, K1, K2tog.

Next Row: Knit the 3 sts together.

Break yarn leaving a length of yarn long enough (8ish inches). to sew up the remaining seam. Fold the cuff over when done sewing.

Make another slipper.

Yes, they do look a little boxy when they're done and not on a foot. The stretch of the garter stitch allows these slippers to stretch around the contours of any foot easily.

Hints and Tips

Picking up the stitch to make the second branch of the antler is sort of up to you. If you pick up the stitch right below where you just knitted, it won't be a disaster. Most deer antlers aren't perfectly symmetrical in real life anyways. In fact, the more off they are, the more desirable; especially if it has a drop tine.

If you want a longer cuff at the top, work more rows than stated at the beginning when you cast on. Make sure to increase the same amount of garter stitch rows and ribbed rows.

When picking up stitches from the cast off row, be sure you're really moving on to the next cast off stitch! It's an easy mistake to pick up a stitch in a stitch you already picked up. If in doubt, give the needle holding the stitches a bit of a tug. You'll see the yarn move slightly at the very back, closest to the needle. Pick up a stitch at the NEXT cast off stitch.

If you don't have the same number of stitches on both sides when you are forming the sole, you may have picked up a stitch twice in one stitch or missed one. Don't worry! This is fixable. You can skip one cast off stitch if you need to make it even, or pick up a cast off stitch twice on the other side. There's enough stretch in the slipper that any puckering this causes won't be overly visible if you're off by a stitch or two.

Picking up the stitches evenly along the toe flap is about 1 stitch every ridge.

To speed up finishing the slippers and not have so many ends to sew in, hold the yarn ends to the back of your work as you knit. You can watch the how to video here - how to work in the ends while knitting these slippers. You can also scan the QR code below.

Abbreviations

K – knit

P - purl

K2tog – knit 2 together

K3tog – knit 3 together

M1 – Make one (knit wise). Increase one stitch between the stitches. Pick up the yarn between the stitches. Twist slightly. Place it on your non-working needle. Knit the stitch. Watch this video to see how.

PM1 - Make one (purl wise). Increase one stitch between the purl stitches. Pick up the yarn between the stitches. Place it on your non-working needle. Purl the stitch as you regularly would. Watch this video to see how.

st – stitch

sts - stitches

Like all of my patterns you have my permission to sell and/or give away the slippers that you make using this pattern. You are NOT permitted to reprint this pattern in any form unless you have obtained my written permission to do so.

If you have any questions, please feel free to leave a comment or send me your questions at kweenbee_crafts@hotmail.ca.

Help Support My Work!

Follow me on <u>Instagram</u>, <u>Facebook</u>, <u>Pinterest</u> and <u>YouTube</u>. Every follow, subscribe, thumbs up, like, heart and share help increase my popularity on the web and get more viewers to my work. It costs you nothing but helps me sooooo much!

If you would like to help a little more, you can always become a <u>Website Member</u> to download and print over 50 patterns. Or you can support me by becoming a Patron on <u>Patreon</u> or you can make a single time donation at <u>Buy Me a Coffee</u>.

You can use any of these QR codes to find out more.

Website Member

Patreon

Buy Me a Coffee

More FREE knitting patterns on my website

I'm always creating new patterns and I post every one of them over on my website. It is an ever growing list so you might want to check out my page at **KweenBee.com**. I design new patterns as I get time. I aim to add a couple new ones each month so the list is always growing!

Below is a VERY small example of the other patterns that I have on the website.

<u>Texting Mittens</u>

<u>Cozy Lace Up Slippers for Adults</u>

<u>Owl Bucket Hat</u>

<u>Winter Beanie Toque or Touque or Tuque with Vertical Stripes</u>

<u>Ultra Thick Slip-On Bootie Slippers</u>

<u>How to Knit a Beanie Hat – with OWLS!</u>

<u>Minimalist Round Toe Slippers</u>

<u>How to Knit a Pair of Flip Mittens or Fingerless Gloves</u>

To make it even easier, you can take a photo of the QR code below with your phone or tablet. A link will pop up. Tap that link and it will take you right to the webpage to see all of the patterns including those above.

You can also do a search for the titles online if QR codes are something that you feel you are unable or don't want to use it.

When you are on your favourite search engine like Google, Bing, Yahoo, etc. Enter the term *Kweenbee* and the title as it is written below (capitalization isn't important). It will pop up for you in the search results and be super-easy to find.

For example, enter it like this:

Your results will have my pattern at the very top...usually. Depending on the popularity of the pattern, you may get a link to Pinterest or Ravelry first. Don't worry! All of those options have links back to my original patterns, too!

Follow Me on Social Media

Take a photo with your phone or tablet of the QR codes below. A link will appear. Click the link to go straight to my social media page.

TikTok	**YouTube**	**Threads**
Facebook	**Instagram**	**Pinterest**
Patreon	**My Etsy Shop**	**Buy Me a Coffee**